Content

Disclaimer

Care and research have been taken
widely to ensure that information
written on this book is as accurate as
possible. But the reader should know
that this information is not a medical,
professional or legal advice and should
not be used for that purpose.

Reading this book demands one to
accept *NO LIABILITY POLICY* for
which the writer is not responsible for
what you do and the outcome of the
knowledge you gain here. This is the

writer's views and expressions regarding Infertility.

Introduction

A lot of people are having difficult conceiving and getting pregnant which makes them visit psychologists and doctors for advice on how to get a child. This is a real stressful struggle to undergo. Most of them are diagnosed for infertility.

According to research infertility is caused by many reasons including; endometriosis, insufficient sperm count ovarian cysts and PCOS among others.

For others this may be caused by more serious issues like obstructed fallopian tubes.

Traditional and using the basic natural ways of solving such complications has been seen to have a higher success rate than the expensive advice from doctors and health specialists.

The modern-day humans tend to focus and trust their doctors more than the natural remedies which if followed correctly can prepare your body for pregnancy with little expenses.

Some prescriptions by specialists have been seen to have a negative impact on one's body including high chances of getting ovarian cancer in ladies compared to the natural holistic methods where you have nothing to lose.

Most of the prescribed drugs have been since to treat the symptoms of infertility rather than treating the main cause of the problem.

This book is mainly focused on teaching people the importance of holistic natural remedies of conceiving as a supplement to health- specialists advice. It gives the readers a chance to get pregnant without drugs or surgeries.

Reason for Infertility in men

It is mostly believed that the main cause for infertility is female related with little knowledge that even men can be the cause of this. According to research, around 37-42% of infertility related cases is male centered.

Most causes of male infertility is less known other than poor sperm mobility which is at least widely studied.

Poor Sperm Mobility

This is caused by a lot of environmental and biological reasons.

Age is an important factor, men less than 40 years of age have a high fertilization rate compared to those of 50 years and above. As of now it stands at 65% fertilization rate for ages 40 and below and 35% for 40 years plus.

More so, factors such as premature ejaculation, impotence and stress can reduce sperm levels too. Mental health awareness, seeking ways to reduce stress and seeking proper guidance against premature ejaculation and impotence is crucial.

Smoking, drug and substance abuse also decreases sperms level and can impair mobile sperms. Men who smoke have low sex drive hence a reduced frequency of sexual activities.

Men with deficiencies in Vitamins; C, folate and selenium are at risk of having a reduced sperm count.

Sperms are repellant to heat so when you overheat your testicles through hot tubs, sauna and undesired underwear can cause low sperm count. Putting on boxer shorts is a great solution for this.

Bicycling is also a cause infertility and impotence because pressure from bike's seat damages nerves and blood vessels which causes erection. This damages the scrotum and testicles hence reduces sperm productivity.

The health and infertility specialists will always prescribe a drug or medication to increase your sperm levels or boost its production but these drugs are the same as those stimulating ovulation. Drugs such as hMG and clomiphene can cause weight gains, damage of liver and blurry vision. Surprisingly there are many natural ways to increase sperm count without use of such drugs with side effects which people don't know about.

Tubular Blockage

Tubular blockages in the epididymis can at times cause men infertility. This is caused by, varicose veins in the testicles, STIs such as Gonorrhea and Chlamydia among others.

Medical specialists recommend surgery to repair varicoceles of which one will have to stay 8 to 10 months to be able to impregnate a woman. Like earlier said there are many natural ways of overcoming this without necessarily getting a surgery.

Non- Specific Infertility

This is where couples can't conceive but nothing specific has been determined as the cause of that. They try to conceive and run tests after another without success.

An infertility specialist normally run several tests including, checking for cysts, sperm quality, tubular blockages or hormonal imbalance and if they can't find anything to link they classify that as non-specific. The couples will then be prescribed infertility drugs such as Clomid hoping that it will make a difference.

They forget that infertility can easily be caused by other factors which frequently don't show symptoms.

Normally human body is supposed to send out signals when something is wrong either by paining or symptoms of where exactly the problem is.

Most pharmaceutical companies have majored their business on treating the symptoms rather than the main cause of the problem.

When you take a pain killer or pain reliever, this is masking your body from the truth. Taking infertility drugs also is trying to hide the fact that something is wrong with your body and needs to be looked at the right way. In some cases, this has been seen to worsen the problem and sometimes making it unbearable or more expensive to treat.

Reasons for Infertility in Women

There are several factors which may make a lady infertile including; 'Lazy' Ovaries, Ovarian Cysts, endometriosis, blockage of fallopian tubes and Polycystic Ovarian Syndrome.

'Lazy' Ovaries

This is where an egg is not released as required by the ovaries. In most cases such patients are prescribed some infertility drugs like Clomid which studies have show that it has more chances of causing ovarian cancer.

According to me ovulation should be stimulated first using natural remedies before seeking specialists help.

Ovarian Cysts

They are fluid filled sacks which develop in the ovaries which are totally harmless. When they rupture and not treated it can be very dangerous and can even cost one's life.

More so, it can interfere with normal conception, though doctors recommend the removal of cysts natural ways of reducing the cysts is recommended because it is less painful than surgeries.

Blockage of fallopian tubes

This is said to account for about 46% of most female infertility cases. The path of sperm to the egg and egg to the uterus is blocked hence no fertilization.

In most cases women don't know if their tubes are blocked. Use of pelvic ultra sound is the most common way of knowing if your fallopian tube is blocked.

Hydrosalpinx and partial blockage are the two types of tube blockages.

Hydrosalpinx of full blockage is when the tube is completely blocked and filled with fluid which makes it dilated and swelled.

Closing off a portion of the tube by endometrial lining causes partial blockage. This leads to ectopic and tubular pregnancies.

Chlamydia, Uterus infection or Pelvic Inflammatory Disease are the most causes of tubular blockages.

Laparoscopic surgery is what specialists suggest for this though I still believe there are some good non-surgical ways to treat this.

Endometriosis

This is where the uterus lining which is suppose to shed regularly during menstrual cycle grows on the outer part of the uterus rather than the inside.

It can cause miscarriages or heavy bleeding during menstrual periods.

Laparoscopic surgery is also advised by the specialists though using traditional herbalists has been used over the years to cure this successfully.

Polycystic Ovarian Syndrome

This is a term given for many small apparent cysts within ovaries. In most cases it is linked to increased resistance to insulin, obesity, lack of ovulation and acne.

Dietary supplement called DCI which is a human metabolite can help treat this.

Understanding Your Body

The human body is a very complex system consisting of several functionalities combined together. Taking in nutritious food gives us the energy to move and perform several tasks.

Human brain is the most complex organ in a human's body. It keeps your body running and co-ordinates functions like heart- beats, breathing, sense of touching among others.

It releases several hormones which enables us to cope with several situations.

There are several hormones released depending with how you feel, hormones releases at your happy times is different from that released when you are sad or disappointed.

For ladies, the enzymes and myriad hormones is what informs the body the right time to release an egg to be able to conceive.

Imagine what would happen when those hormones are not released at the right time and in right proportions?

One may be tempted to visit a doctor for such where they will be prescribed a drug which regulates the hormones. These drugs sometimes can cause complications or interfere with your well-functioning body.

Treat your body like a car, if your put the wrong gas into the fuel tank there is a high chance that it may fail to work. If you put water instead of gasoline there is 90% chance it won't start.

It is important to think about what you take each day to make sure everything performs well.

You should focus on eating nutritious food rather than eating food to sustain yourself from time to time.

Understanding what you eat and take in to your body is important to improve your infertility state and treatment if any. You should only eat the advised food type to increase the chances of conceiving.

Replacing junk unhealthy food with greens, fruits or any organic food can be crucial. Alcohol, drugs, caffeine and nicotine can also affect your ability to naturally conceive and alters your body's ability to function well.

Understanding reasons and importance of every nutrient you plan to add on your diet is important in making sure what you do brings out positive results.

According to research high levels of stress is linked to infertility in women. Testosterone is released to a woman's system when stress levels increases.

They become upset, aggressive and moody hence are unable to cope with pressure and stress.

A counter-reactive release of oxytocin in women is needed to combat stress and bring back a loving and caring state of mind.

Effective ways of dealing with stress is crucial in reversing infertility. High levels of testosterone in the body reduces chances of pregnancy hormones to perform right.

Toxins Elimination

At this time and age, exposure to toxins and chemicals which are poisonous may be harmful to your health.

If you were told that the shampoo you use to clean your hair is harmful and affects your fertility rate will you change it? Will another shampoo have the same effects?

Have you ever taught about the effects of things we use on day to day basis like toothpaste, conditioners or colognes?

Most of these substances are said to increase toxicity levels in the body some having long term effects and others short.

Foods to Avoid

Eliminating certain food types from your body while trying to conceive is crucial if you want to have a baby.

Fact has it that caffeine intake reduces your fertility levels by up to 52%. Immediate thinking may push you to cut or reduce coffee intake but that is not enough. There is a lot of substances taken which contains caffeine so cutting down on intake of one substance is not sufficient to sort this problem.

Soda, pain relievers and chocolates also contain caffeine, excessive intake of these will hormonal imbalance and ovulation rate.

Alcohol levels in your body also affects your fertility levels. It is advisable to reduce alcohol intake as much as possible when trying to conceive preferably around 4-5 months before you conceive.

Improving your diet ensures that your body generates the right levels of hormones needed to make you healthy and improves your response to treatments.

Taking a walk for around 30 minutes each day counts, this will boost your endorphins levels and also increases levels of Vitamin D in your body.

Eating nutritious foods, minerals and having correct vitamins intake has a lot of health benefits to you. This creates the right environment to nurture and keep an embryo hence improves the chances of getting pregnant naturally.

According to medical studies, reduced menstrual crumps and ovarian cysts is a result of healthy diet.

Foods to Add

Simple food stuffs like legumes, vegetables, nuts and fruits have a great impact on your body as far as conceiving is concerned.

Having a good immune system is important when trying to conceive and eating foods rich in Vitamin B and those containing folic acid can help boost your immunity.

Folic acid prevents some birth related complications like miscarriages and spina bifida.

Avocado, green leaves, papaya, eggs, beans, nuts and oranges are some good sources of Folic acid and Vitamin B.

Those with low levels of Zinc in the body are subjected to reduced infertility rates hence intake of Oysters may have a great impact on this.

Sex talk

A lot of information exists out there about sex and how to do it right to get pregnant but most of them are actually false or misleading information. Some are told that having sex during your cycle can make you pregnant which is not true.

About 2-3 days before you ovulate is the right time to have sex to increase your chances of getting pregnant because this is the time where a lady is most fertile.

The problem now is knowing exactly when your ovulation period starts.

Normally a menstrual cycle lasts for 28 days, day one being the beginning of your periods, some specialists have it that ovulation is on the 14th day of your menstrual cycle so many have sex on day 14 to increase the chances of conceiving. The problem is that every woman's cycle and ovulation period varies hence making this approach not to work for everybody.

Basal temperature kids and ovulation predictors are some accurate ways to predict your ovulation. They are available in most pharmacies.

The best way to predict your most fertile window is when you notice the most fertile cervical mucus discharge.

Cervical mucus is the clear, sticky and raw egg white discharge from a lady's vagina. Having sex at this time is important because this mucus will ensure the sperms swim and survive in a more effective manner.

Timing when to have Sex

If you are planning to conceive, having sex twice a week regardless of the signs will increase the connection between the two of you and ability of getting pregnant.

Timing when to have sex is not the way to go if you are trying to get pregnant because for males, the sperm quantity and quality only peaks after one or two days of abstinence so if he waits for more days, the quality and quantity needed for optimum fertility mat be affected.

According to research, women who have orgasm have a high chance of getting pregnant because, spasmodic contraction of the uterus pulls the sperm deep into the uterus rather than leaking out of the vagina.

Sex position

Some sex positions are believed to increase the chances of getting pregnant than others. Any position can make you pregnant but some are believed to increase the chances of conceiving than others.

If a woman likes it on top this the chances of getting pregnant are low since sperms may leak out of the system easily.

For those who like exploring more, missionary style is the best position if you are trying to conceive.

To ensure the sperm has a swift flow to the lady one is advised not to immediately get up after sex, that may wipe or easily remove sperm from the vagina.

Those with tipped uterus should try doggy style.

Boy or Girl

There is a lot of misinformation about the sex of your unborn child regarding sex time, food you eat or sex position.

Most of them are not biologically proven.

Men produce sperm Y and X. The faster small Y sperm becomes male while slower X sperm becomes female.

There is no a specific way to determine gender of your child but you can favor your odds for certain preferred sex.

Having a Girl

If you want to have a girl you should try to have sex around 7 days before ovulation and then severally until after ovulation then avoid sex until ovulation ends.

Ideally, small faster Y sperm will reach the uterus and die earlier before even the egg is released but larger slower X sperms may still be serving until ovulation.

A shallow penetration is also said to increase chances of having a girl. The pH levels in the vagina counts. An acidic environment will kill weak Y sperm faster leaving the X sperms hence increasing their chances of fertilization.

Deeper penetration increases the chances of faster sperms to reach their destination faster.

If you want a girl it may be better for you not to reach an orgasm because the body releases substances which makes the body more alkaline hence reduces chances of getting a girl.

Having a Boy

When you want a boy it is important not to have sex until around 1-3 days before ovulation which should be followed by a consecutive sexual activities until after ovulation.

Deep penetration and having an orgasm is important to deposit sperms closer to the cervix for faster swimming and to increase number of sperms going to the cervix respectively.

Conclusion

There is no one sure way of curing infertility, but there are many ways to make it possible to conceive.

Addressing what you can control can be of great importance to improve your chances of conceiving.

You should focus on trying natural methods of trying to conceive before going for other alternatives.